Removing the mask
(Who are you at your core?)

S. Rivers
Santiego Rivers

Removing the mask

(Who are you at your core?)

Copyright © 2021 by **Santiego Rivers**

All rights reserved. This book may not be reproduced or transmitted in any form without the written permission of the author.

ISBN 978-1-7370516-5-7

We all wear a mask that we show the world, which becomes the veil that hides and protects us from the eyes and opinions of the judgmental world we live in.

We become so comfortable wearing the mask that we forget to remove it when we are around people whom we love, cherish and adore because of the fear and insecurities that made us put the mask on in the beginning.

We get so caught up in pretending that we forget how to live and love at the moment we are in love. As a result, the fantasy of whom we want people to see and admire becomes more accurate than the reality of who we are at our core.

Yes, we are dual nature creatures, but at our core, we are one unique special being that we hide and deny our self the opportunity to get to know, hiding behind our mask.

Being Unapologetic:

There will be pain, heartache, and tears when we finally decide to remove the mask and introduce the world to the authentic version of ourselves.

In the beginning, you will regret your decision to remove your veil because you will lose many people who are not ready to accept you for who you are but don't give in to the feeling of regret.

It takes rain to produce the rainbow to guide you on your path. Everyone in your life is not supposed to accept you for who you are. The most important thing is that you learn to embrace the person you are and want to be moving forward.

Your life is yours to live. Your life is not meant for you to spend your time trying to impress people you do not even like.

That statement goes for friends, family members, and even loved ones because the only people you will ever need in your life are the ones who will challenge you to become your best, even when you have your doubts.

Life will teach you many valuable lessons if you are willing to learn. You will discover many lessons even if you are not ready to understand them. Sometimes you must be willing to lose the world just for the opportunity to reclaim your soul.

It would be best to learn to smile from the inside so that smile on your face accurately represents how you feel within your soul.

Removing the mask
(Who are you at your core?)

I remember when I first put on my mask to shield the parts of me that I did not think the world would accept. Who would ever believe that the reason that you needed a mask as a youth is to fit in with your family?

Your own family as a youth is the society that helps shape and mold you for better or for worse.

I was the youngest child of my mother. I had an older brother who was my role model in my youth, for better or worse.

I wanted to be like my brother growing up, so I tried to follow in his footsteps. He loved sports, so I liked sports. When he got into trouble, I got into trouble too.

I was an introvert pretending to be an extrovert not to have to face my biggest fear. But, of course, my biggest fear was being me.

I enjoyed singing, writing poetry, reading mystery books, playing with my action figures, and just being alone.

It would take me years to embrace or be comfortable being the person the Most High designed me to be.

To be or not to be, they say that this is the question that we should always ask ourselves. I feel the only question that we should want to know is who are we not to be great?

Living behind my mask was tough. I was always in a constant battle with myself. I dueled with who I was pretending to be versus who I was as a person.

For a short time, I removed my mask as a youth and revealed who I was as a person. My reintroduction occurred when my cousins came to stay with my brother and me because their parents were having issues.

Their connection reminded me of my brother and me but in reverse. Lil Frank, the youngest of the brothers, reminded me of my older brother Tony.

He was more outgoing and did not mind getting into trouble.

Warren, the oldest brother, had a beautiful soul. He was the person that I could connect with more as a child.

He allowed me the opportunity to open and nourish the gifts that I had inside as a writer. He copied my writings and allowed me to create a book of my work that I still have to this very day.

Warren had good handwriting compared to mine. But, unfortunately, my penmanship was not that good if you asked the people who made it necessary for me to start wearing my mask as a child.

It felt good not to hide behind a mask anymore and be the person I wanted to be.

When my cousins went home, I found myself putting back on my mask not to be alone or afraid to be myself.

Wearing that mask for me was tough. It brought on depression, anger, and other bad feelings that made it easy for me to hate myself.

I avoided looking into the mirror because I never saw my true reflection in the mirror. Instead, I saw the mask that I wore that I thought would be more pleasing to the world.

The sacrifices that we often make to please others make it hard for us to be comfortable in our own skin.

I became a great pretender fooling everyone but myself. It would take me many years to learn to ask myself this one simple question:

who am I trying to impress?

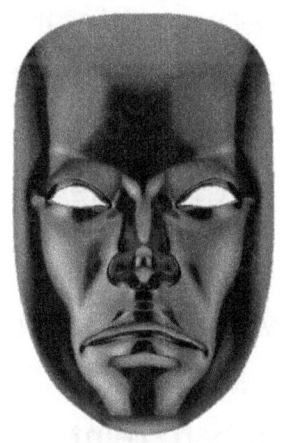

If we create all the monsters and obstacles that we put in our lives, we have the power and the ability to remove and destroy them all.

It would take me a long time to understand the following quote and how to apply it to my life.

The Most High did not give us the spirit of fear. He blessed us with power, love, and that of a sound mind." – **2 Timothy 1:7**

That version of the quote is my interpretation of the quote and how I was able to understand it. We must interpret the world around us to help it make sense to us for our growth and development as a person.

I continued to wear my mask in high school until I met my friend Charles. He allowed me the opportunity to reintroduce myself to my true self.

He was not an athlete in high school. Charles and I connected more on an intellectual level.

We both enjoyed writing poetry and learning. However, I admit that it felt good not to pretend to enjoy what everyone likes doing.

Charles and I wrote poems that allowed us to create a book of poetry. I think that we challenged each other to become solid writers.

In my youth, my poetry writing was more about rhyming, where Charles's writing would paint pictures with his words which I would later adapt into my style as a writer.

It felt great to be around someone who challenged me for the best. I am a firm believer that you can predict your future by identifying your friends.

In high school, I was living two lives. On the one hand, I was an all-American jock living the dream, while on the other hand, I was the nerdy young adult who wondered why we dream?

Meeting Charles put a big dilemma in my life. Do I continue to be the all-American jock, or do I spend more time getting to know my true self and develop my skills?

For a very long time, I did both. I liked the popularity that being a jock brought me, and I loved my ability to develop my talents with Charles.

I went to college utilizing my talent as an athlete and my gifts as a writer. I had an athletic scholarship and an academic scholarship to attend Delaware State University.

Living two lives made my transition into adulthood difficult. The more that I fought with myself made it easy for me to lash out at the world and the people around me.

I would continue this battle deep into adulthood until I dared to live life in front of the mask.

Removing the mask
(Who are you at your core?)

What will it take for a person to stop living behind the mask and show the world their true reflection?

Your reason for taking off the mask must be greater than the reason that you put the mask on in the first place.

It is difficult for anyone to change a behavior or pattern without replacing it with something else. So, what will be the courage you need to replace your fears?

For me, it was being tired of not living up to my full potential and being unhappy in the process.

The one question that I ask anyone who I feel needs to make a change in their life is the following:

How is your life working out for you?

You can lie to other people, but it is difficult to lie to yourself when you are the only audience in attendance.

Removing the mask
(Who are you at your core?)

For many years, I hid behind my mask because the people around me made me feel that being me was not enough.

I wondered that being me was not enough for whom? Was it not enough for a child who felt something when other people were in denial about feeling anything that did not suit their purpose?

Was it not beneficial to admit that I had a calling on my life, but you could not see it in me because you felt that you gave me life? Or maybe it was because you thought since we grew up in the same household, I couldn't be great because you felt that you were not great yourself?

As I mentioned earlier, sometimes, your family can make you feel more comfortable hiding behind the mask.

A child would never understand unless someone teaches them that the only person who must approve of who they are is themselves.

We all are intelligently designed to be like no one else. We all matter! We are not a mistake because the Most High does not make mistakes.

Our life has meaning and purpose. It is up to you to find the meaning and the purpose of your life.

In discovering your purpose, you may wonder what if the new direction in your life does not agree with the people in your life currently? It will then be time to find a new set of people to surround yourself with in your new life.

Your circle of people is supposed to complete you and help develop your growth as a person.

Developing into the best version will require you to lose people who do not support or encourage your growth.

Family members should never be exempt from this equation. But, unfortunately, most people who wear masks or have issues that they struggle with can easily trace their problems back to the people who were supposed to love and protect them.

The people who broke them mentally sent them out into the world as damaged goods.

Those damaged goods became incapable of having a healthy relationship with other people because of the damage that love ones have caused them. This hurt has forced them to wear the mask longer than they should have.

The years of mental abuse have made them feel that if the people who were supposed to love them did not make them feel loved, how could they ever get what they need from anyone else?

I have seen people throw away their marriages because of the opinion and the doubts that their mental abuser had put inside their head.

Those people spend their adult years trying to create a relationship with the same people who broke them as a child.

Common sense would teach us if common sense were common that you will never have the same relationship with people from your childhood now that you are grown.

Make the people from your childhood respect you as an adult and not the broken and scared child you once were.

Seek respect instead of seeking love. If you love yourself, nothing else matters.

You will never get what you deserve if you keep holding onto all the things you don't deserve.

Remove yourself from people and situations that are not healthy for you. When you become too busy worrying about everything that you will lose, removing people and things from your life, you forget all the things you will gain by finally having peace in your life.

Stop chasing a moment in life from your past before you miss out on the other moments in your life that matters the most.

The past is meant for reflection and to measure how far you have come. The present and the future hold all the possibilities of tomorrow.

Are you willing to remove the mask and live in the moment which is now?

Your mindset should be the following to find the courage to remove the mask from the equation:

> *I would rather you hate me for who I am than to love me for who I am not.*

A wise man knows and understands that making a sacrifice is required to grow. What sacrifices are you willing to make to grow?

A better question is, what are you willing to fight for to obtain happiness in your life? Life will give you what you fight for or you settle for in the end.

What will you fight for, or will you choose to settle for the world that the mask presents you to?

www.ingramcontent.com/pod-product-compliance
Lightning Source LLC
Chambersburg PA
CBHW071014160426
43193CB00012B/2055